Presented to:

From:

Date:

THE ILLUSTRATED WESTMINSTER SHORTER CATECHISM

IN MODERN ENGLISH

P.O.BOX 817 • PHILLIPSBURG • NEW JERSEY 08865-0817

The text of the Westminster Shorter Catechism is taken from Douglas Kelly and Philip Rollinson, *The Westminster Shorter Catechism in Modern English* (Phillipsburg, NJ: Presbyterian and Reformed Publishing Company, 1986). It has been updated with the ESV and lightly modernized.

ISBN: 978-1-62995-974-0 (hbk)
ISBN: 978-1-62995-950-4 (ePub)

Printed in the United States of America

Library of Congress Cataloging-in-Publication Data has been applied for.

To my children:

May this book be a tool
of growth in the knowledge
of our Lord and Savior,
Jesus Christ.

And these words that I command you today shall be on your heart. You shall teach them diligently to your children, and shall talk of them when you sit in your house, and when you walk by the way, and when you lie down, and when you rise. You shall bind them as a sign on your hand, and they shall be as frontlets between your eyes.

Deuteronomy 6:6–8

Contents

Introduction

The Westminster Shorter Catechism is a series of questions and answers designed to teach the basic biblical doctrines of the Christian faith. Written by a group of men known as the Westminster Assembly, it was completed in 1647 and has been used in the church ever since.

Question 1

What is man's primary purpose?

Answer

Man's primary purpose is to glorify God and to enjoy him forever.

Ps. 73:25–26; Rom. 11:36; 1 Cor. 10:31

Question 2

What authority from God directs us how to glorify and enjoy him?

Answer

The only authority for glorifying and enjoying God is the Bible, which is the Word of God and is made up of the Old and New Testaments.

Luke 16:31; 24:27, 44; John 15:11; Gal. 1:8–9; 2 Tim. 3:16–17; 2 Peter 3:2, 15–16

Question 3

What does the Bible primarily teach?

Answer

The Bible primarily teaches what man must believe about God and what God requires of man.

John 5:39; 20:31; Rom. 15:4; 1 Cor. 10:11; 1 John 1:3–4

Question 4

What is God?

Answer

God is a spirit, whose being, wisdom, power, holiness, justice, goodness, and truth are infinite, eternal, and unchangeable.

Gen. 17:1; Ex. 3:14; 34:6–7; Pss. 90:2; 145:3; John 4:24; Rom. 11:33; James 1:17; Rev. 4:8

Question 5

Is there more than one God?

Answer

There is only one—the living and true God.

Deut. 6:4; Jer. 10:10; John 17:3; 1 Cor. 8:4

Question 6

How many persons are in the one God?

Answer

Three persons are in the one God: the Father, the Son, and the Holy Spirit. These three are one God, the same in substance and equal in power and glory.

Matt. 3:16–17; 28:19; John 1:1; 5:18; Acts 5:3–4; 2 Cor. 13:14; Heb. 1:3

Question 7

What are the decrees of God?

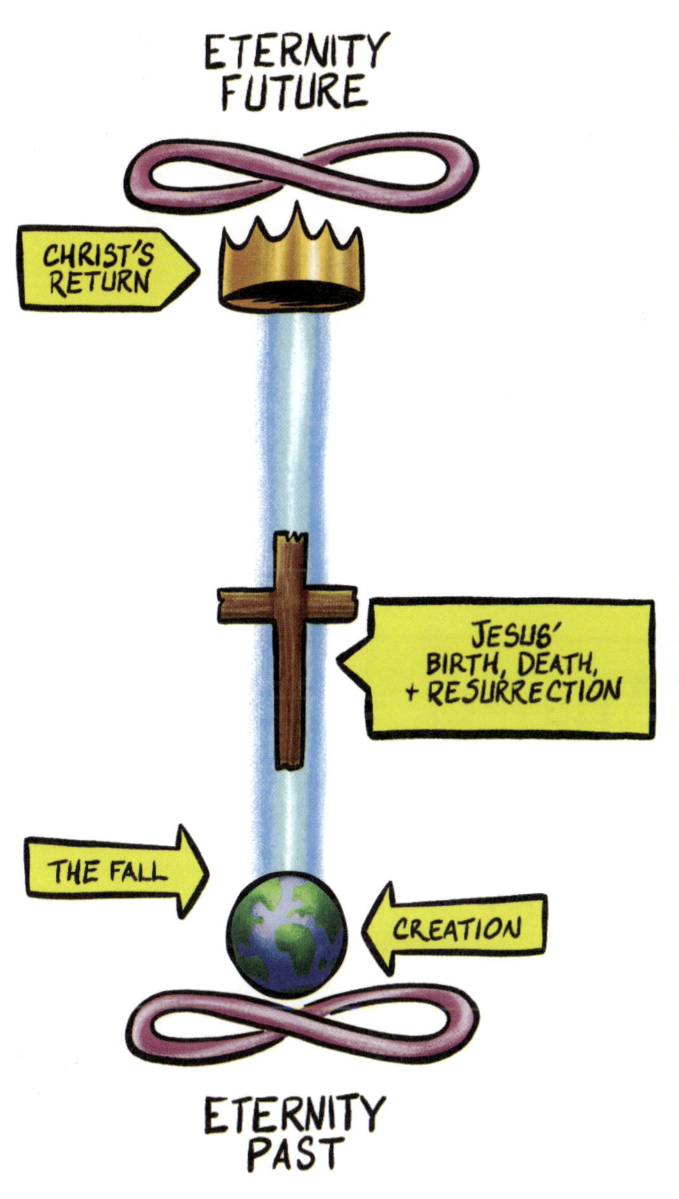

Answer

The decrees of God are his eternal plan based on the purpose of his will, by which, for his own glory, he has foreordained everything that happens.

Acts 2:23; Rom. 11:36; Eph. 1:11

Question 8

How does God carry out his decrees?

Answer

God carries out his decrees in creation and providence.

Isa. 40:26; Dan. 4:35; Rev. 4:11

Question 9

What is creation?

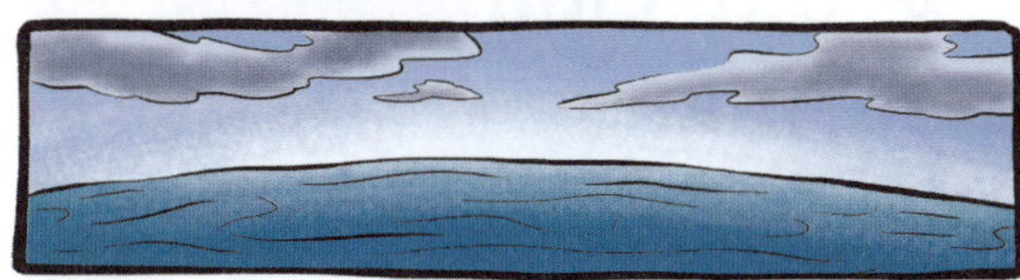

Answer

Creation is God's making everything out of nothing by his powerful Word in six days—and all very good.

Gen. 1:1, 31; Ps. 33:9; Heb. 11:3

Question 10

How did God create man?

Answer

God created man—male and female—in his own image and in knowledge, righteousness, and holiness, to rule over the other creatures.

Gen. 1:27–28; Eph. 4:24; Col. 3:10

Question 11

What is God's providence?

Answer

God's providence is his completely holy, wise, and powerful preserving and governing every creature and every action.

Neh. 9:6; Pss. 104:24; 145:17; Matt. 10:30; Heb. 1:3

Question 12

What did God's providence specifically do for man whom he created?

Answer

After the creation, God made a covenant with man to give him life if he perfectly obeyed; God told him not to eat from the Tree of Knowledge of Good and Evil or he would die.

Gen. 2:17; Gal. 3:12

Question 13

Did our first parents remain as they were created?

Answer

Left to the freedom of their own wills, our first parents sinned against God and fell from their original condition.

Gen. 3:6; Rom. 5:12

Question 14

What is sin?

Answer

Sin is disobeying or not conforming to God's law in any way.

Rom. 4:15; James 2:10; 4:17; 1 John 3:4

Question 15

By what sin did our first parents fall from their original condition?

Answer

Our first parents' sin was eating the forbidden fruit.

Gen. 3:12–13

Question 16

Did all mankind fall in Adam's first disobedience?

Answer

Since the covenant was made not only for Adam but also for his natural descendants, all mankind sinned in him and fell with him in his first disobedience.

Gen. 1:28; Acts 17:26; 1 Cor. 15:21–22

Question 17

What happened to man in the fall?

Answer

Man fell into a condition of sin and misery.

Rom. 5:12–13

Question 18

What is sinful about man's fallen condition?

Answer

The sinfulness of that fallen condition is twofold. First, in what is commonly called original sin, there is the guilt of Adam's first sin with its lack of original righteousness and the corruption of his whole nature. Second are all the specific acts of disobedience that come from original sin.

Rom. 5:18–19; 8:7–8; Eph. 2:1

Question 19

What is the misery of man's fallen condition?

Answer

By their fall, all mankind lost fellowship with God and brought his anger and curse on themselves. They are therefore subject to all the miseries of this life, to death itself, and to the pains of hell forever.

Gen. 3:8, 24; Mark 9:47–48; Rom. 6:23; Eph. 2:3

Question 20

Did God leave all mankind to die in sin and misery?

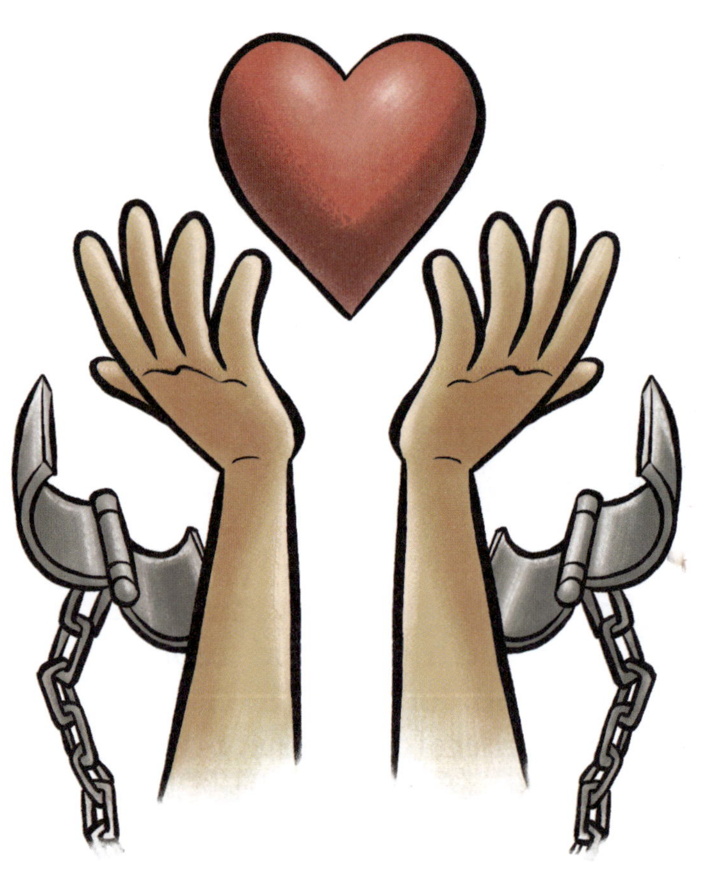

Answer

From all eternity and merely because it pleased him, God chose some to have everlasting life. These he freed from sin and misery by a covenant of grace and brought to salvation by a redeemer.

John 17:6; Eph. 1:4; Titus 1:2; 3:7

Question 21

Who is the Redeemer of God's chosen ones?

Answer

The only Redeemer of God's chosen is the Lord Jesus Christ, the eternal Son of God, who became man. He was and continues to be God and man in two distinct natures and one person forever.

John 1:14; Rom. 9:5; Col. 2:9; 1 Tim. 2:5; Heb. 13:8

Question 22

How did Christ, the Son of God, become man?

Answer

Christ, the Son of God, became man by assuming a real body and a reasoning soul. He was conceived by the power of the Holy Spirit in the womb of the Virgin Mary, who gave birth to him, yet he was sinless.

Matt. 26:38; Luke 1:31, 35; 2:52; Heb. 2:14; 4:15

Question 23

How is Christ our Redeemer?

Answer

As our Redeemer, Christ is a prophet, priest, and king in both his humiliation and his exaltation.

Ps. 2:6; John 1:49; Acts 3:22; Heb. 5:5–6

Question 24

How is Christ a prophet?

Answer

As a prophet, Christ reveals the will of God to us for our salvation by his Word and Spirit.

John 1:18; 14:26; 16:13; Heb. 1:1–2

Question 25

How is Christ a priest?

Answer

As a priest, Christ offered himself up once as a sacrifice for us to satisfy divine justice and to reconcile us to God, and he continually intercedes for us.

Rom. 3:26; 10:4; Heb. 2:17; 7:25; 9:28

Question 26

How is Christ a king?

Answer

As a king, Christ brings us under his power, rules and defends us, and restrains and conquers all his and all our enemies.

Ps. 110:3; Acts 2:36; 18:9–10

Question 27

How was Christ humiliated?

Answer

Christ was humiliated by being born as a man and born into a poor family; by being made subject to the law and suffering the miseries of this life, the anger of God, and the curse of death on the cross; and by being buried and remaining under the power of death for a time.

Isa. 53:3; Matt. 27:46; Luke 2:7; 1 Cor. 15:3–4; Gal. 3:13; 4:4; Phil. 2:7–8

Question 28

How is Christ exalted?

Answer

Christ is exalted by his rising from the dead on the third day, his going up into heaven, his sitting at the right hand of God the Father, and his coming to judge the world at the last day.

Acts 17:31; 1 Cor. 15:4; Eph. 1:20

Question 29

How are we made to take part in the redemption Christ bought?

Answer

We take part in the redemption Christ bought when the Holy Spirit effectively applies it to us.

John 1:12; 3:5–6; Titus 3:5–6

Question 30

How does the Holy Spirit apply to us the redemption Christ bought?

Answer

The Spirit applies to us the redemption Christ bought by producing faith in us and so uniting us to Christ in our effective calling.

Gal. 2:20; Eph. 4:15–16

Question 31

What is effective calling?

Answer

Effective calling is the work of God's Spirit, who convinces us that we are sinful and miserable, who enlightens our minds in the knowledge of Christ, and who renews our wills. This is how he persuades and makes us able to receive Jesus Christ, who is freely offered to us in the gospel.

Ezek. 36:26–27; John 6:37, 44–45; Acts 2:37; 26:18; Phil. 2:13; 2 Thess. 2:13

Question 32

What benefits do those who are effectively called share in this life?

Answer

In this life, those who are effectively called share justification, adoption, sanctification, and the other benefits that either go with or come from them.

Rom. 8:30; 1 Cor. 1:30; Eph. 1:5

Question 33

What is justification?

Answer

Justification is the act of God's free grace by which he pardons all our sins and accepts us as righteous in his sight. He does so only because he counts the righteousness of Christ as ours. Justification is received by faith alone.

Rom. 3:24; 4:6; 5:18; 2 Cor. 5:21; Gal. 2:16; Eph. 1:7

Question 34

What is adoption?

Answer

Adoption is the act of God's free grace by which we become his sons with all the rights and privileges of being his.

John 1:12; Rom. 8:17; 1 John 3:1

Question 35

What is sanctification?

Answer

Sanctification is the work of God's free grace by which our whole person is made new in the image of God and we are made more and more able to become dead to sin and alive to righteousness.

Rom. 6:6; Eph. 4:24; 1 Peter 1:2

Question 36

What benefits in this life go with or come from justification, adoption, and sanctification?

Answer

The benefits that in this life go with or come from justification, adoption, and sanctification are the assurance of God's love, peace of conscience, joy in the Holy Spirit, and growing and persevering in grace to the end of our lives.

John 1:16; Rom. 5:1–2, 5; 14:17;
Phil. 1:6; 1 Peter 1:5

Question 37

What benefits do believers receive from Christ when they die?

Answer

When believers die, their souls are made perfectly holy and immediately pass into glory. Their bodies, which are still united to Christ, rest in the grave until the resurrection.

Luke 23:43; John 5:28; Acts 7:55, 59; 2 Cor. 5:8; Phil. 1:23; 1 Thess. 4:14; Rev. 14:13; 19:8

Question 38

What benefits do believers receive from Christ at the resurrection?

Answer

At the resurrection, believers, raised in glory, will be publicly recognized and declared not guilty on the day of judgment and will be made completely happy in the full enjoyment of God forever.

Ps. 16:11; Matt. 10:32; 25:34; 1 Cor. 15:43

Question 39

What does God require of man?

Answer

God requires man to obey his revealed will.

Mic. 6:8; Luke 10:28

Question 40

What rules did God first reveal for man to obey?

Answer

The rules he first revealed were the moral law.

Rom. 2:14–15

Question 41

Where is the moral law summarized?

Answer

The moral law is summarized in the Ten Commandments.

Deut. 10:4; Matt. 19:17

Question 42

What is
the essence of the
Ten Commandments?

Answer

The essence of the Ten Commandments is to love the Lord our God with all our heart, with all our soul, with all our strength, and with all our mind and to love everyone else as we love ourselves.

Matt. 22:37–40

Question 43

What introduces the Ten Commandments?

Answer

These words introduce the Ten Commandments: "I am the Lord your God, who brought you out of the land of Egypt, out of the house of slavery."

Ex. 20:2

Question 44

What does the introduction to the Ten Commandments teach us?

Answer

The introduction to the Ten Commandments teaches us that, because God is Lord and is our God and Redeemer, we must keep all his commandments.

Deut. 11:1; 1 Peter 1:17–19

Question 45

What is the first commandment?

Answer

The first commandment is "You shall have no other gods before me."

Ex. 20:3

Question 46

What does the first commandment require?

Answer

The first commandment requires us to know and recognize God as the only true God and our God and to worship and glorify him accordingly.

Deut. 26:17; 1 Chron. 28:9; Ps. 95:6–7; Matt. 4:10

Question 47

What does the first commandment forbid?

Answer

The first commandment forbids denying God or not worshipping and glorifying him as the true God and our God. It also forbids giving worship and glory, which he alone deserves, to anyone or anything else.

Pss. 14:1; 81:9–10; 97:7; Rom. 1:20–21, 25

Question 48

What are we specifically taught in the first commandment by the words "before me"?

Answer

The words "before me" in the first commandment teach us that God, who sees everything, notices and is very offended by the sin of having any other god.

Deut. 30:17–18; Ps. 139:1–3

Question 49

What is the second commandment?

Answer

The second commandment is "You shall not make for yourself a carved image, or any likeness of anything that is in heaven above, or that is in the earth beneath, or that is in the water under the earth. You shall not bow down to them or serve them, for I the Lord your God am a jealous God, visiting the iniquity of the fathers on the children to the third and the fourth generation of those who hate me, but showing steadfast love to thousands of those who love me and keep my commandments."

Ex. 20:4–6

Question 50

What does the second commandment require?

Answer

The second commandment requires us to receive, respectfully perform, and preserve completely and purely all the regulations for religion and worship that God has established in his Word.

Deut. 12:32; Matt. 28:20

Question 51

What does the second commandment forbid?

Answer

The second commandment forbids our worshipping God with images or in any other way not established in his Word.

Rom. 1:22–23; Col. 2:18

Question 52

What are the reasons for the second commandment?

Answer

The reasons for the second commandment are that God totally rules over us, that we belong to him, and that he is eager to be worshipped correctly.

Ex. 34:14; Pss. 45:11; 100:3; 1 Cor. 10:22

Question 53

What is the third commandment?

Answer

The third commandment is "You shall not take the name of the Lord your God in vain, for the Lord will not hold him guiltless who takes his name in vain."

Ex. 20:7

Question 54

What does the third commandment require?

HOLINESS
SOVEREIGNTY
OMNISCIENT
FATHER
ADONAI
OMEGA

Answer

The third commandment requires the holy and reverent use of God's names, titles, qualities, regulations, Word, and works.

Pss. 29:2; 104:24; 138:2; Eccl. 5:1; Rev. 15:3–4

Question 55

What does the third commandment forbid?

Answer

The third commandment forbids our treating as unholy or abusing anything God uses to make himself known.

Lev. 19:12; Matt. 5:34–35

Question 56

What is the reason for the third commandment?

Answer

The reason for the third commandment is that the Lord our God will not allow those who break this commandment to escape his righteous judgment, although they may escape punishment from men.

Deut. 28:59

Question 57

What is the fourth commandment?

Answer

The fourth commandment is "Remember the Sabbath day, to keep it holy. Six days you shall labor, and do all your work, but the seventh day is a Sabbath to the Lord your God. On it you shall not do any work, you, or your son, or your daughter, your male servant, or your female servant, or your livestock, or the sojourner who is within your gates. For in six days the Lord made heaven and earth, the sea, and all that is in them, and rested on the seventh day. Therefore the Lord blessed the Sabbath day and made it holy."

Ex. 20:8–11

Question 58

What does the fourth commandment require?

Answer

The fourth commandment requires us to set apart to God the times he has established in his Word—specifically one whole day out of every seven as a holy Sabbath to him.

Lev. 19:30; Deut. 5:12

Question 59

Which day of the week has God designated as the Sabbath?

Answer

From the beginning of the world until the resurrection of Christ, God established the seventh day of the week as the Sabbath. From that time until the end of the world, the first day of the week is the Christian Sabbath.

Gen. 2:3; Ex. 16:23; Acts 20:7; 1 Cor. 16:1–2; Rev. 1:10

Question 60

How do we keep the Sabbath holy?

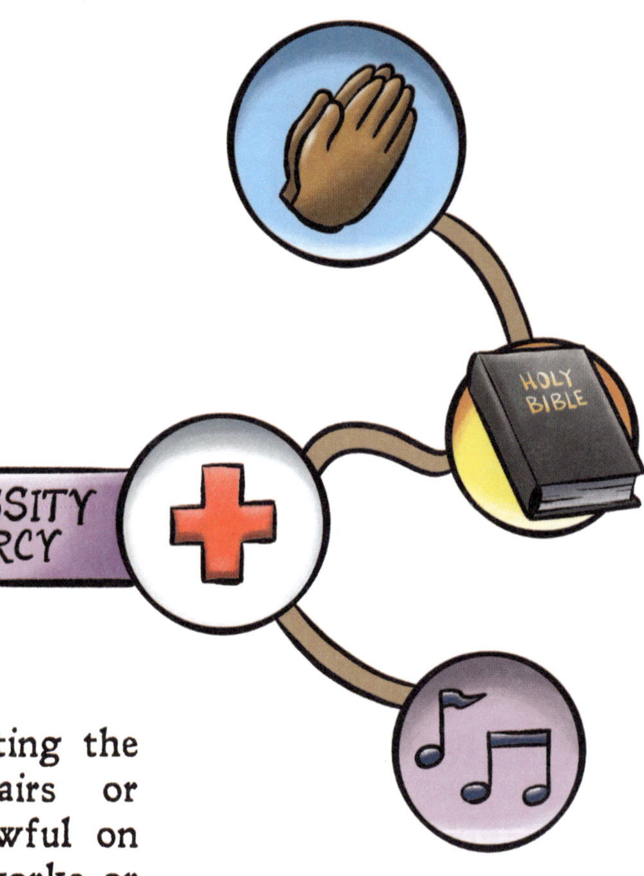

Answer

We keep the Sabbath holy by resting the whole day from worldly affairs or recreations, even ones that are lawful on other days. Except for necessary works or acts of mercy, we should spend all our time publicly and privately worshipping God.

Lev. 23:3; Isa. 58:13–14; Matt. 12:11–12; Mark 2:27

Question 61

What does the fourth commandment forbid?

Answer

The fourth commandment forbids failing to do or carelessly doing what we are supposed to do. It also forbids treating the day as unholy by loafing, by doing anything in itself sinful, or by unnecessary thinking, talking about, or working on our worldly affairs or recreations.

Jer. 17:21; Ezek. 23:38; Luke 23:56

Question 62

What are the reasons for the fourth commandment?

Answer

The reasons for the fourth commandment are these: God allows us six days of the week to take care of our own affairs; he claims the seventh day as his own; he set the example; and he blesses the Sabbath.

Gen. 2:3; Ex. 31:15–17; Lev. 23:3

Question 63

What is the fifth commandment?

Answer

The fifth commandment is "Honor your father and your mother, that your days may be long in the land that the Lord your God is giving you."

Ex. 20:12

Question 64

What does the fifth commandment require?

Answer

The fifth commandment requires us to respect and treat others—whether above, below, or equal to us—as their position or our relationship to them demands.

Lev. 19:32; Rom. 12:10; 13:1; Eph. 6:1, 5, 9

Question 65

What does the fifth commandment forbid?

Answer

The fifth commandment forbids being disrespectful to or not treating others as their position or relationship to us demands.

Rom. 13:7–8

Question 66

What is
the reason for the
fifth commandment?

Answer

The reason for the fifth commandment is the promise of long life and prosperity, if these glorify God and are for the good of those who obey this commandment.

Eph. 6:2–3

Question 67

What is the sixth commandment?

Answer

The sixth commandment is "You shall not murder."

Ex. 20:13

Question 68

What does the sixth commandment require?

Answer

The sixth commandment requires making every lawful effort to preserve one's own life and the lives of others.

Ps. 82:3–4; Eph. 5:29–30

Question 69

What does the sixth commandment forbid?

Answer

The sixth commandment forbids taking one's own life or the lives of others unjustly or doing anything that leads to suicide or murder.

Gen. 9:6; Deut. 24:6; Prov. 24:11–12; Acts 16:28; 1 John 3:15

Question 70

What is the seventh commandment?

Answer

The seventh commandment is "You shall not commit adultery."

Ex. 20:14

Question 71

What does the seventh commandment require?

Answer

The seventh commandment requires us and everyone else to keep sexually pure in heart, speech, and action.

Eph. 4:29; 5:11–12; 1 Thess. 4:4; 2 Tim. 2:22; 1 Peter 3:2

Question 72

What does the seventh commandment forbid?

Answer

The seventh commandment forbids thinking, saying, or doing anything sexually impure.

Matt. 5:28; Eph. 5:3–4

Question 73

What is the eighth commandment?

Answer

The eighth commandment is "You shall not steal."

Ex. 20:15

Question 74

What does the eighth commandment require?

Answer

The eighth commandment requires that we lawfully acquire and increase our own and others' money and possessions.

Lev. 25:35; Deut. 15:10; Prov. 27:23

Question 75

What does the eighth commandment forbid?

Answer

The eighth commandment forbids anything that either does or may unjustly take away money or possessions from us or anyone else.

Prov. 28:19; 1 Tim. 5:8; James 5:4

Question 76

What is the ninth commandment?

Answer

The ninth commandment is "You shall not bear false witness against your neighbor."

Ex. 20:16

Question 77

What does the ninth commandment require?

Answer

The ninth commandment requires us to tell the truth and to maintain and promote it and our own and others' reputations, especially when testifying.

Prov. 14:5, 25; Acts 25:10; Eph. 4:25; 1 Peter 3:16; 3 John 12

Question 78

What does the ninth commandment forbid?

Answer

The ninth commandment forbids anything that gets in the way of the truth or injures anyone's reputation.

Pss. 12:3; 15:3; 2 Cor. 8:20–21; Col. 3:9

Question 79

What is the tenth commandment?

Answer

The tenth commandment is "You shall not covet your neighbor's house; you shall not covet your neighbor's wife, or his male servant, or his female servant, or his ox, or his donkey, or anything that is your neighbor's."

Ex. 20:17

Question 80

What does the tenth commandment require?

Answer

The tenth commandment requires us to be completely satisfied with our own status in life and to have a proper, loving attitude toward others and their possessions.

Lev. 19:18; 1 Cor. 13:4–6; 1 Tim. 6:6; Heb. 13:5

Question 81

What does the tenth commandment forbid?

Answer

The tenth commandment forbids any dissatisfaction with what belongs to us, envy or grief at the success of others, and all improper desire for anything that belongs to someone else.

1 Cor. 10:10; Gal. 5:26; Col. 3:5

Question 82

Can anyone perfectly keep the commandments of God?

Answer

Since the fall, no ordinary human being can perfectly keep the commandments of God in this life but breaks them every day in thought, word, and action.

Rom. 3:9–10; 8:8; James 3:2

Question 83

Are all sins equally evil?

Answer

In the eyes of God, some sins in themselves are more evil than others, and some are more evil because of the harm that results from them.

Ps. 19:13; Matt. 11:24; Luke 12:10; Heb. 10:29

Question 84

What does every sin deserve?

Answer

Every sin deserves God's anger and curse, both in this life and in the life to come.

Matt. 25:41; Gal. 3:10; James 2:10

Question 85

What does God require from us to escape his anger and curse, which we deserve for our sin?

Answer

To escape God's anger and curse, which we deserve for our sin, God requires from us faith in Jesus Christ and repentance unto life along with diligent involvement in all the external ways Christ uses to bring us the benefits of redemption.

Acts 20:21; 1 Tim. 4:16; Heb. 2:3; 2 Peter 1:10

Question 86

What is faith in Jesus Christ?

Answer

Faith in Jesus Christ is a saving grace, by which we receive and rest on him alone for salvation, as he is offered to us in the gospel.

John 1:12; Acts 16:31; Phil. 3:9; Heb. 10:39; Rev. 22:17

Question 87

What is repentance unto life?

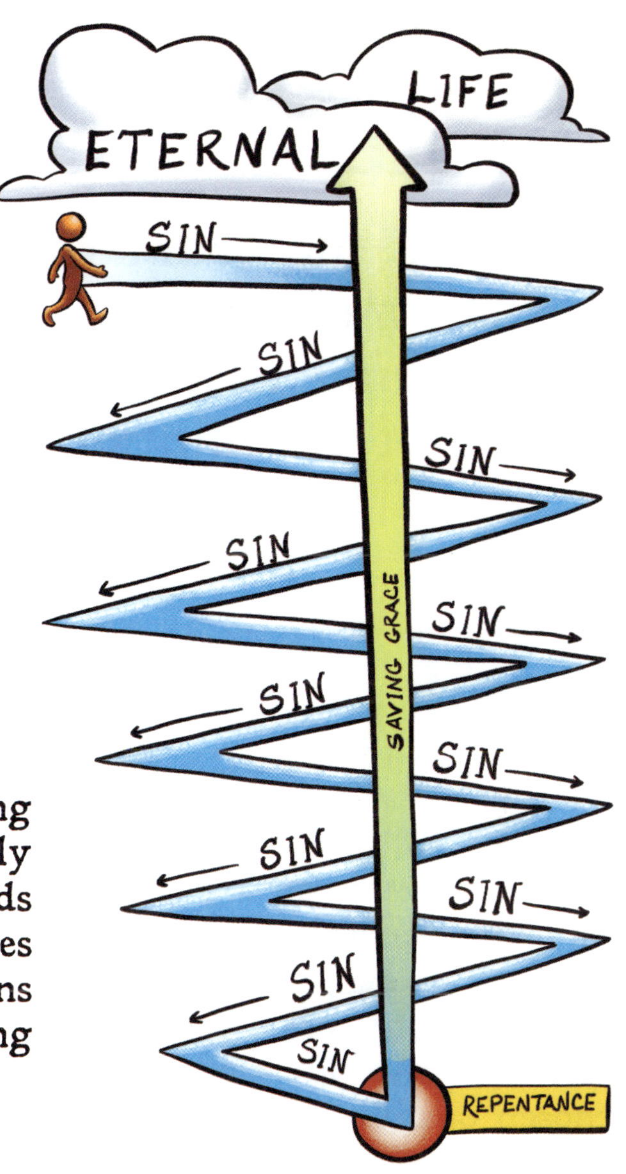

Answer

Repentance unto life is a saving grace, by which a sinner, being truly aware of his sinfulness, understands the mercy of God in Christ, grieves for and hates his sins, and turns from them to God, fully intending and striving for a new obedience.

Jer. 31:18–19; Luke 1:77–79; Acts 2:37; Rom. 6:18; 2 Cor. 7:10

Question 88

What are the ordinary, external ways Christ uses to bring us the benefits of redemption?

Answer

The ordinary, external ways Christ uses to bring us the benefits of redemption are his regulations—particularly the Word, sacraments, prayer—all of which are made effective for the salvation of his chosen ones.

Acts 2:41, 42

Question 89

What makes the Word effective for salvation?

Answer

The Spirit of God causes the reading and especially the preaching of the Word to convince and convert sinners and to build them up in holiness and comfort through faith to salvation.

Neh. 8:8; Acts 20:32; Rom. 15:4; 2 Tim. 3:15; James 1:21

Question 90

How is the Word to be read and heard in order to become effective for salvation?

Answer

For the Word to become effective for salvation, we must pay careful attention to it, prepare ourselves, and pray for understanding. We must also receive it with faith and love, treasure it in our hearts, and practice it in our lives.

Deut. 6:6–7; Ps. 119:11, 18; Rom. 1:16; 2 Thess. 2:10; James 1:25; 1 Peter 2:1–2

Question 91

How do the sacraments become effective means of salvation?

Answer

The sacraments become effective means of salvation not because of any special power in them or in the people who administer them but rather by the blessing of Christ and the working of his Spirit in those who receive them by faith.

Rom. 2:28–29; 1 Cor. 12:13; 1 Peter 3:21

Question 92

What is a sacrament?

Answer

A sacrament is a holy regulation established by Christ, in which Christ and the benefits of the new covenant are represented, sealed, and applied to believers by physical signs.

Matt. 26:26–28; 28:19; Rom. 4:11

Question 93

What are the sacraments of the New Testament?

Answer

The sacraments of the New Testament are baptism and the Lord's Supper.

Acts 10:47–48; 1 Cor. 11:23–26

Question 94

What is baptism?

Answer

The sacrament of baptism is a washing with water in the name of the Father, the Son, and the Holy Spirit, which is a sign and seal that we are joined to Christ, that we receive the benefits of the covenant of grace, and that we are engaged to be the Lord's.

Matt. 28:19; John 3:5; Rom. 6:3, 5; Gal. 3:27

Question 95

Who should be baptized?

Answer

Those who are not members of churches should not be baptized until they have publicly stated that they believe in Christ and will obey him, but the infant children of church members should be baptized.

Gen. 17:7, 10; Acts 2:38–39; 18:8; 1 Cor. 7:14

Question 96

What is the Lord's Supper?

Answer

The Lord's Supper is a sacrament in which bread and wine are given and received as Christ directed to proclaim his death. Those who receive the Lord's Supper in the right way share in his body and blood with all his benefits—not physically but by faith—and become spiritually stronger and grow in grace.

Luke 22:19–20; 1 Cor. 10:16; 11:23–26

Question 97

What is the right way to receive the Lord's Supper?

Answer

The right way to receive the Lord's Supper is to examine whether we discern the Lord's body, whether our faith feeds on him, and whether we have repentance, love, and a new obedience—so that we may not come in the wrong way and eat and drink judgment on ourselves.

Rom. 6:17–18; 1 Cor. 11:27, 31–32

Question 98

What is prayer?

Answer

Prayer is offering our desires to God in the name of Christ for things that agree with his will, confessing our sins, and thankfully recognizing his mercies.

Pss. 10:17; 145:19; John 16:23; Phil. 4:6; 1 John 1:9; 5:14

Question 99

How does God direct us to pray?

Answer

The whole Word of God—but especially the Lord's Prayer, which Christ taught his disciples—directs our prayers.

Ps. 119:170; Matt. 6:9–13; Rom. 8:26

Question 100

What does the beginning of the Lord's Prayer teach us?

Answer

The beginning of the Lord's Prayer ("Our Father in heaven") teaches us to draw near to God with completely holy reverence and confidence, as children to a father who is able and ready to help us. It also teaches that we should pray with and for others.

Luke 11:13; Rom. 8:15; 1 Tim. 2:1–2

Question 101

For what do we pray in the first request?

Answer

In the first request ("hallowed be your name"), we pray that God will enable us and others to glorify him in everything he uses to make himself known and that he will work out everything to his own glory.

Ps. 67:1–3; Rom. 11:36; Rev. 4:11

Question 102

For what do we pray in the second request?

Answer

In the second request ("Your kingdom come"), we pray that Satan's kingdom may be destroyed, that the kingdom of grace may be advanced, with ourselves and others brought into and kept in it, and that the kingdom of glory may come quickly.

Ps. 68:1; Matt. 9:37–38; John 12:31; Rom. 10:1; 2 Thess. 3:1; Rev. 22:20

Question 103

For what do we pray in the third request?

Answer

In the third request ("your will be done, on earth as it is in heaven"), we pray that by his grace God would make us have the capability and the will to know, obey, and submit to his will in everything, as the angels do in heaven.

Ps. 103:20–21; Matt. 26:39; Phil. 1:9–11

Question 104

For what do we pray in the fourth request?

Answer

In the fourth request ("Give us this day our daily bread"), we pray that we may receive an adequate amount of the good things in this life as a free gift of God and that with them we may enjoy his blessing.

Prov. 10:22; 30:8–9; 1 Tim. 6:6–8

Question 105

For what do we pray in the fifth request?

Answer

In the fifth request ("forgive us our debts, as we also have forgiven our debtors"), encouraged by God's grace, which makes it possible for us sincerely to forgive others, we pray that for Christ's sake God would freely pardon all our sins.

Ps. 51:1–2, 7; Matt. 18:35; Mark 11:25

Question 106

For what do we pray in the sixth request?

Answer

In the sixth request ("And lead us not into temptation, but deliver us from evil"), we pray that God would either keep us from being tempted to sin or support and deliver us when we are tempted.

Ps. 19:13; Matt. 26:41; John 17:15; 1 Cor. 10:13

Question 107

What does the conclusion of the Lord's Prayer teach us?

Answer

The conclusion of the Lord's Prayer ("For yours is the kingdom and the power and the glory forever") teaches us to be encouraged only by God in our prayers and to praise him by acknowledging that kingdom, power, and glory are his. To show that we want to be heard and have confidence that we are, we say, "Amen."

1 Chron. 29:11–13; Dan. 9:18–19; 1 Cor. 14:16; Phil. 4:6; Rev. 22:20–21

And God spoke all these words, saying, "I am the Lord your God, who brought you out of the land of Egypt, out of the house of slavery."

Exodus 20:1–2

The Ten Commandments

1 You shall have no other gods before me.

2 You shall not make for yourself a carved image, or any likeness of anything that is in heaven above, or that is in the earth beneath, or that is in the water under the earth. You shall not bow down to them or serve them, for I the Lord your God am a jealous God, visiting the iniquity of the fathers on the children to the third and the fourth generation of those who hate me, but showing steadfast love to thousands of those who love me and keep my commandments.

3 You shall not take the name of the Lord your God in vain, for the Lord will not hold him guiltless who takes his name in vain.

4 Remember the Sabbath day, to keep it holy. Six days you shall labor, and do all your work, but the seventh day is a Sabbath to the Lord your God. On it you shall not do any work, you, or your son, or your daughter, your male servant, or your female servant, or your livestock, or the sojourner who is within your gates. For in six days the Lord made heaven and earth, the sea, and all that is in them, and rested on the seventh day. Therefore the Lord blessed the Sabbath day and made it holy.

5 Honor your father and your mother, that your days may be long in the land that the Lord your God is giving you.

6 You shall not murder.

7 You shall not commit adultery.

8 You shall not steal.

9 You shall not bear false witness against your neighbor.

10 You shall not covet your neighbor's house; you shall not covet your neighbor's wife, or his male servant, or his female servant, or his ox, or his donkey, or anything that is your neighbor's.

The Lord's Prayer

Our Father in heaven,
hallowed be your name.
Your kingdom come,
your will be done,
on earth as it is in heaven.
Give us this day our daily bread,
and forgive us our debts,
as we also have forgiven our debtors.
And lead us not into temptation,
but deliver us from evil.

For yours is the kingdom and the power and the glory forever. Amen.

The Apostles' Creed

I believe in God the Father Almighty, Maker of heaven and earth:

And in Jesus Christ his only Son, our Lord; who was conceived by the Holy Ghost, born of the Virgin Mary, suffered under Pontius Pilate, was crucified, dead, and buried; he descended into hell; the third day he rose again from the dead; he ascended into heaven, and sits on the right hand of God the Father Almighty; from there he shall come to judge the living and the dead.

I believe in the Holy Spirit; the holy catholic church; the communion of saints; the forgiveness of sins; the resurrection of the body; and the life everlasting.

Amen.

And Jesus came and said to them, "All authority in heaven and on earth has been given to me. Go therefore and make disciples of all nations, baptizing them in the name of the Father and of the Son and of the Holy Spirit, teaching them to observe all that I have commanded you. And behold, I am with you always, to the end of the age."

Matthew 28:18–20

Notes